MW00943881

CRUISE PACKING

MADE EASY

Stress-free and ready to relax

Kyler Ayim

Disclaimer

I am not affiliated with any cruise line or travel agency, nor am I employed by or compensated by them to publish any content found in this book or the marketing of this book.

The information in this book has been researched and presented to the best of my ability. However, I make no guarantee on the accuracy of the information.

Each cruise line will have its own guidelines for which items are allowed on board their ships. Your luggage will be put through security and/or customs checks so please follow the policies of your cruise line, airline, and transportation security administration.

table of contents

Introduction 1

Cruise Packing Preparation 3

Clothing: What To Wear And How Much To Bring . . . 6

Packing Checklist 33

Carry-on Tips & Checklist 37

Packing Tips & Advice 42

Accessories to Make Life Easier 49

What Not to Pack 55

Conclusion 61

more secure, but it's harder to sync between devices. For offline password managers I suggest Password Safe or KeePass.

Tips / Gratuities

Many cruise ships distribute tips to all the staff based on some formula, and simply charge this amount to your credit card. This is not voluntary, but written into your contract with the company. However, if you want to tip anyone who has been extra helpful then prepare a handful of bills for tipping on the cruise, at the hotel, and along the way. If you want you can calculate the recommended amounts of gratuity before your trip and withdraw money in the proper denominations in advance.

Check Your Luggage

OK, now it's time to get out your luggage and check its condition. You're looking for tears as well as testing the locks and zippers. Also check to see if anything spilled inside on an earlier trip. Decide whether your luggage is good to go, in need of repairs, or in need of replacement.

CLOTHING:
WHAT TO WEAR AND
HOW MUCH TO BRING

What to wear, what to wear? Some days it can be hard to choose what to wear even when you don't have to account for various weather, activities, multiple days, and limited space.

This chapter covers the following topics:
- Dress For Your Destination
- Cruise Wear Slideshow
- Cruise Line Dress Codes
- How To Pack Fewer Clothes
- Common Clothing Questions

Dress For Your Destination

Some things you're going to pack no matter what (hello underwear!), but sometimes you'll want particular clothing items depending on where you're going or what you're doing. Planning ahead can make things so much easier! In addition to the destination advice below, I suggest looking up what kind of activities you'll want to do on the cruise ship and during shore excursions so that you know what you'll need to wear for those.

Here are some tips to help you dress for your destination.

Alaska (can also apply to Scandinavian / Nordic cruises)
- Forecast: Fluctuating temperatures and surprise rain showers.
- Layers! People who live in places with spring/fall temperature swings know the power of dressing in layers. For example: an undershirt, t-shirt, fleece, and a windbreaker jacket. If you're cold, wear them all, and if things get warmer then take off a layer.
- You don't have to go into full winter-mode, but items like warm hat and gloves, earmuffs, light jackets, and scarves are useful. If you want to make sure you're warm, long johns or thermal underwear are a good idea too. You're not just battling the cold, but the wind too.
- Alaska gets a lot of rain, especially May through September, so you'll want an umbrella plus a raincoat or poncho. It's best if the rain jackets have a hood and space for layers underneath. If your footwear isn't completely waterproof (or even if it is), bringing extra socks for excursions is a good way to plan ahead.
- Speaking of excursions, Alaska is known for its rugged terrain. Pick up a pair of hiking boots or sturdy shoes. Even if they're already waterproof some people like to spray them with a weather protector shoe spray.
- While a folding or collapsible bag isn't a clothing item, it's useful for holding the layers you shed as the day heats up.
- If you want to pack lighter, it's possible to buy an outer jacket in port. I've read a number of comments from cruisers saying they liked the jackets they bought in Alaska.
- If you do buy a jacket specifically for the cruise, one suggestion is to buy it a little large so that you have room for layers

underneath. And remember to leave space in your suitcase to bring the new purchase home.

- Ketchikan, AK is often mentioned as the best place to buy, but check your itinerary because if that's your last port it won't do you much good!

Caribbean

- Forecast: Hot days and cool nights (unless you're dancing!)
- These locations tend to be more casual than the norm.
- Since you'll likely be spending a lot of time in swimwear, pack 2 or 3 swimsuits so you can rotate them as needed.
- Unless you want peeling skin tomorrow and wrinkles later in life, bring sunscreen and a hat to protect yourself from the sun. There are plenty of styles to choose from; just make sure the brim is wide enough to provide shade for your face and ears.
- Warm clothing is often forgotten on tropical cruises. Many areas of the ship may have the AC on full blast, and a light sweater or fashionable scarf/wrap can prevent you from getting chilled during dinner. Plus the weather could get cool enough that you wish you had something warmer for outside too, especially at night.
- Speaking of the weather, it does rain in the tropics (despite what all the postcards show!). A poncho, rain jacket or windbreaker, and even a small umbrella will come in handy to keep you from getting soaked.

European

- Forecast: This one's hard to summarize because of the variety of climates. So do your due diligence and plan ahead based on whether you'll be cruising Scandinavia, the UK, the Mediterranean, etc.

- To over-generalize, European cruises tend to be more formal so bring some resort casual attire (read: dressier casual).
- Scout out which tourist attractions you want to visit because some historic or religious sites have stricter dress codes. If you want to visit these locations bring something to cover your shoulders and knees such as a shawl, light sweater, pants, or over-the-knee skirts.

Exotic (e.g. Africa, Asia, Middle East, and more!)

- In the Middle East or other conservative-leaning destinations, women may need to wear a headscarf to cover their hair and/or wear clothes that cover their arms and legs, even if it's warm out.
- If you'll be in the jungle, you'll want long sleeves and pants to prevent bug bites. Insect repellent is good too and should contain DEET if you want to be sure it works. It's also possible to find clothing that's been treated to repel mosquitoes. You can even buy "invisible" mosquito netting for your hat to protect your face and neck.
- They may not be the most fashionable, but pants with zippers that convert into shorts are the definition of "function over fashion" when dealing with changes in temperature or the possible need to wear pants to enter a place of worship.

Cruise Wear Slideshow

I don't know about you, but for me, seeing examples of something is really helpful. So here is a photo gallery of people on cruises and excursions. You may need to zoom in for some of these photos.

Onboard: Warm or Sunny Days

Onboard: Mild Days

"DSC00695, Interior of Celebrity Cruise Ship Century" by Jim G is licensed under CC BY 2.0

Onboard: Poolside

PHOTO BY COREY ANN ON VISUALHUNT.COM / CC BY-ND

Onboard: Chilly Days

Onboard: Casual Eveningwear

Onboard: Formal Eveningwear

"DSC01203, Dinner on the Century, Somewhere at Sea" by Jim G is licensed under CC BY 2.0

"Formal Photo on Family Cruise in Miami" by Mark Krynsky is licensed under CC BY 2.0

Onboard: Theme Nights

In-Port Attire: Tropical

In-Port Attire: Arctic

"HIKING" BY CHRISTINE RONDEAU IS LICENSED UNDER CC BY 2.0

In-Port Attire: European

"DSC00733, GAMLA STAN, STOCKHOLM, SWEDEN" BY JIM G IS LICENSED UNDER CC BY 2.0

"DSC00720, GAMLA STAN, STOCKHOLM, SWEDEN" BY JIM G IS LICENSED UNDER CC BY 2.0

In-Port Attire: Conservative

"Taj Mahal" by Rool Paap is licensed under CC BY 2.0

Cruise Line Dress Codes

In this subsection I'll summarize the dress codes of various cruise lines to give you a combined general description.

Cruise line dress codes have become less formal over the last few decades. Nowadays appropriate daytime clothing is described with terms such as terms like "resort casual" and "country club casual". Some companies fully embrace a "casual and comfortable" approach to daytime attire so on many ships you'll be fine with just a t-shirt and shorts; or if you want to go a little nicer then try golf/polo shirts, khakis, capris, casual skirts or dresses, pants/slacks.

Swimsuits are appropriate for the pool areas but are rarely permitted in the dining room. Speedos are not very common except in parts of Europe, and bikinis aren't great for water slides or other activities where you might accidentally expose yourself.

Evenings tend to be a little more formal but unless it's a scheduled "formal night" typical descriptions include phrases like "elegant casual" and "smart casual and above". Depending on your cruise line you can go a little more or less formal. Options include summer dresses, dress shorts, non-cutoff jeans, blouses, collared shirts of various types, and slacks.

For the scheduled formal nights, first take note of your cruise itinerary to see how many there are, if any. Shorter cruises may have just one formal night, cruises of around seven days could have about two, and longer cruises may have two or three or even more depending on the length of the cruise. Then again, some cruises don't have any formal nights at all!

So check your ship's schedule and you'll know how many formal nights there are and the suggested attire. Descriptions often include cocktail dresses, pantsuits, elegant skirts, dress shirts and dress pants. Feel free to get dressed to the nines if you'd like but ties and jackets are generally not required unless specifically stated. However, it's good to check because some lines do recommend that passengers dress up in evening gowns or suits and tie for special events.

If there's more than one formal night on your cruise you don't necessarily have to pack multiple formal outfits. Turn one suit/dress into many by using different accessories like scarves, jewelry, and ties.

How To Pack Fewer Clothes

Two keys for efficient packing are: multiple use items and finding ways to bring less. To help achieve both of these objectives, let's talk about creating a mix & match wardrobe and doing laundry on the ship.

Create a mix and match wardrobe

The general idea here is to plan ahead so you can rewear pants/skirts with different tops. For example, you could wear a top to dinner that's been dressed up with accessories (jewelry, scarves, etc.) and then reuse that same shirt more casually later on during a shore excursion.

The next level to the mix & match idea is to choose a color theme and coordinate one or two colors throughout your wardrobe. This makes it easier to match clothes, meaning you can bring less and not have to remember which tops/bottoms were planned to go together in a certain outfit. Simply mix and match!

This goes for shoes as well. If you choose footwear that can match anything then all you need is a comfortable pair for the daytime and a dressier pair for the evenings.

Tip: If you have the self-discipline to work out during a cruise, and your athletic shoes are bulky, it's better to wear them during travel and pack the smaller shoes. (By the way, see the **Packing Tips & Advice** chapter for efficient shoe packing ideas.)

If you don't mind wearing the same outfit twice, you can pack even less! Your fellow passengers probably won't even notice, and if they do they probably don't care. Anyway, do you really care if they do care?

> *"You probably wouldn't worry about what people think of you if you could know how seldom they do!"* — *Olin Miller*

Finally, another way to lighten your load is to pack (or buy) clothing made from microfiber. This fabric is lightweight and also low-maintenance so it dries quickly and resists wrinkles. On top of that, microfiber wicks away moisture and has stain-repellent qualities, which means fewer clothing changes due to sweat or accidental spills.

Laundry
I know, I know . . . Doing laundry is probably one of the last things a person wants to do while on vacation.

However, the fact of the matter is that laundering your cruise wear means you can pack less in the first place. No matter how good at packing we may be, there's no trick or hack that will make a piece of clothing smaller or lighter than simply not bringing it.

So then the question is: hand wash or machine wash?

Most big ships offer some kind of laundry service, but what exactly they provide varies. Sometimes you can buy a laundry package before the cruise, other times you can pay per laundry bag, and sometimes you even have access to self-service washing machines. If you can, catch the laundry specials (check the bulletin) and take advantage of freebies offered in the loyalty program.

For hand washing, here are a few tips:
- There is detergent made specifically for hand washing.
- The Scrubba wash bag is like a travel-sized washing machine that provides a quick and quality wash.

- Drying after hand washing can be difficult, especially in inside cabins, but the trick is to wring the clothes out well then roll them in a dry towel to get out even more moisture. Those ShamWow towels are great for this.
- Inflatable hangers dry out clothes faster because they separate the fabrics allowing air to flow.
- Air circulation is key. Hang wet clothes near doors, air vents, or even bring a travel fan to blow air around.
- For gently worn clothes just use a travel-sized bottle of fabric refresher spray.

Even with all these tips, some items are better for handwashing on a cruise than others. Lighter fabrics like underwear, swimsuits, and lightweight tops seem to dry out well enough, but heavier clothes like jeans or 100% cotton may take forever to dry in a cabin.

You might not be able to hand wash everything, but even washing a few items can certainly reduce your laundry bill!

Common Clothing Questions

Below I answer a few questions that haven't already been addressed elsewhere in this chapter.

Can I wear shorts or jeans in the dining room?

For dinner, many cruise lines allow you to wear jeans that aren't ripped up, but shorts are usually frowned upon. Things are more relaxed for breakfast and lunch, so you can probably wear shorts in the morning or afternoon.

Check with your specific cruise company for their guidelines.

Do I have to dress up on theme nights?
No. Even though many cruises have theme nights ranging from "Glow Party" to "Mexican Fiesta" to "Pirate Night", they are optional. Some cruisers go all out with a full body costume, others just wear a fancy hat, and some just go to people-watch.

What shoes should I bring?
This is a greatly debated subject among cruisers. Some people pack light and manage to do just fine with a couple of pairs of shoes. Others want a pair for every occasion.

If you choose footwear that can match anything then all you need is a comfortable pair for the daytime and a dressier pair for the evenings.

If you want to cover more situations, then consider the following:
- Flip flops or boat shoes during the day (although flip flops are usually not allowed in the dining room)
- Dress shoes, heels, nice sandals or flats for the evenings
- Sneakers, walking shoes, or hiking boots for port excursions or sightseeing tours

PACKING CHECKLIST

Y ou don't have to pack every single item on this list. The idea here is to check off items as you pack them so that you don't forget anything important. This checklist is flexible, meaning that the length of your cruise will determine, for example, how many shirts you'll want to bring. Simply skip over anything you won't need.

Note: Some items you may choose to put in your carry-on instead, especially in the Accessories and Toiletries categories. It mostly comes down to personal preference.

To download this checklist as a PDF, go to: kylerayim.com/cruise/packing-checklist.pdf

The Essentials
- Passports and/or Visas
- Photo ID (Driver's License or State Issued ID)
- Tickets (Flight and Cruise)
- Booking Confirmations
- Trip Itinerary
- Travel Health Insurance (International)

- Purse or Handbag
- Credit/Debit Card and Cash

Clothing

- Underwear
- Socks
- Undershirts / Bras
- Sleepwear / Pajamas
- T-Shirts
- Dress Shirts / Collared Shirts
- Swimwear / Cover-ups
- Jeans
- Pants / Trousers
- Shorts
- Dresses / Skirts / Summer Dress
- Formal Wear
- Shoes (see Footwear section)
- (Cold Destinations) Hats, Scarves, Gloves, Coats
- Work out gear
- Jacket
- Rash Shirt
- Cardigans
- Kaftan / Kimono
- Beach Hat
- Long Sleeve Shirts
- Tank Tops
- Rainwear
- Sweaters / Sweatshirts

Don't Forget the Kids

- Seasonal Clothing
- Travel Pack

- Electronic Devices w/ Chargers & Extra Batteries
- Children's Medications
- Swim Wear / Floaties / Goggles
- Favorite Toys / Blanket / Stuffed Animal

Toiletries
- Toothbrush, toothpaste, mouthwash, floss
- Deodorant / Perfume
- Sea sickness tablets
- Medications & Vitamins/Supplements
- Small First Aid Kit
- Sunscreen
- Moisturizer / Face Lotion / Gels / Etc.
- After-bite cream / Insect repellent
- Hand Sanitizer
- Soap / Shower Gel
- Shaving Supplies: Razor blades, shaving cream
- Tweezers / Nail File Clippers
- Comb / Hairbrush
- Glasses (and case) / Contacts lenses & solution
- Feminine hygiene products
- Shampoo and conditioner
- Make-up / Make-up Remover

Accessories
- Plug adapters
- Cell phone, plus charger
- Gorilla pod or Selfie stick
- Laptop or tablet, plus charger
- Portable music device, plus charger
- Headphones
- Water bottle

- Hairdryer
- Eye Mask
- Earplugs
- Money Pouch / Cross Body Bag / Backpack
- Collapsible Totes
- Binoculars

Activities
- Electronics, plus charger
- Journal or notepad
- Pens
- Playing cards
- Books / eBooks / Magazines

Footwear
- Leisure Shoes
- Hiking / Athletic Shoes
- Walking Shoes
- Dress Shoes
- Sandals / Flip-flops
- Slippers (Night Shoes)

To download this checklist as a PDF, go to: kylerayim.com/cruise/packing-checklist.pdf

CARRY-ON TIPS & CHECKLIST

Most people are familiar with a carry-on bag for air travel, but they exist for cruise travel as well. When you are first boarding the ship, you'll leave your main luggage with the porters and walk onto the ship with your carry-on. Just like a flight, you'll be without your luggage for a period of time (until it's delivered to your room). However, unlike a flight, you aren't stuck in a single seat for hours … you have an entire ship to explore!

This is why a cruise carry-on requires special attention.

The following tips will help you prepare your carry-on so you're ready for your first day on the ship. After the tips there's a Cruise Carry-On Checklist for you.

Checked Luggage vs Carry-on

Valuables and important items stay with you, either on your person or in your carry-on. Checked luggage isn't the place for passports, daily medicine, jewelry, cameras and electronics, travel documents, etc. Once you're on your way, the same goes for car keys and parking claim checks.

By the way, carry-on restrictions for airlines vary between companies and could have changed since the last time you flew. Consult their guidelines before packing and heads up that purses sometimes count as a carry-on item.

In Case of Lost Luggage

Have some clothes and items for the first day on the ship before your luggage is delivered to your room. This way if your luggage has trouble finding its way back to you, you'll still be able to go swimming or have appropriate clothes for the dining room. At the minimum pack in your carry-on a change of clothes and whatever toiletries and accessories you can't live without. In fact, it's safest to just pack your carry-on like it's the only bag coming with you, because in a worst-case scenario it would be!

Pro tip: Some cruise lines will give you a voucher to purchase items from their store. So if your luggage goes missing, go report it to the front desk. No guarantee but it doesn't hurt to ask!

Cruise Carry-On Checklist

You don't have to pack every single item on this list. The idea here is to check off items as you pack them so that you don't forget anything important. This checklist is flexible, meaning that the length of your cruise will determine, for example, how many shirts you'll want to bring. Simply skip over anything you won't need.

To download this checklist as a PDF, go to: kylerayim.com/cruise/carry-on-checklist.pdf

The Essentials
- Passports and/or Visas
- Photo ID (Driver's License or State Issued ID)
- Tickets (Flight and Cruise)
- Booking Confirmations
- Trip Itinerary
- Travel Health Insurance (International)
- Purse or Handbag
- Credit/Debit Card and Cash
- Maps / Directions
- Medical Insurance Card
- Emergency Contacts
- Camera
- Cell Phone

Clothes & Footwear
- Underwear
- Socks
- Undershirts / Bras
- Sleepwear / Pajamas
- T-Shirts
- Dress Shirts / Collared Shirts
- Swimwear / Cover-ups
- Jeans
- Pants / Trousers
- Shorts
- Dresses / Skirts / Summer Dress
- Formal Wear
- Shoes (Dress Shoes, Sandals, Sneakers, Walking Shoes)
- (Cold Destinations) Hats, Scarves, Gloves, Coats
- Work out gear
- Jacket

- Rash Shirt
- Cardigans
- Kaftan / Kimono
- Beach Hat
- Long Sleeve Shirts
- Tank Tops
- Rainwear
- Sweaters / Sweatshirts

Toiletries

- Toothbrush, toothpaste, mouthwash, floss
- Deodorant / Perfume
- Sea sickness tablets
- Medications & Vitamins/Supplements
- Sunscreen
- Moisturizer / Face Lotion / Gels / Etc.
- First-Aid Ointment, Bandages
- After-bite cream / Insect repellent
- Hand Sanitizer
- Soap / Shower Gel
- Shaving Supplies: Razor blades, shaving cream
- Tweezers / Nail File Clippers
- Comb / Hairbrush
- Glasses (and case) / Contacts lenses & solution
- Feminine hygiene products
- Shampoo and conditioner
- Make-up / Make-up Remover
- Pain Reliever

Accessories

- Plug adapters
- Cell phone, plus charger

- Gorilla pod or Selfie stick
- Laptop or tablet, plus charger
- Portable music device, plus charger
- Headphones
- Water bottle
- Hairdryer
- Eye Mask
- Earplugs
- Money Pouch / Cross Body Bag / Backpack
- Collapsible Totes

Miscellaneous
- Chewing Gum / Food / Snacks
- Books / eBooks / Magazines
- Travel Pillow / Blanket

To download this checklist as a PDF, go to: kylerayim.com/cruise/carry-on-checklist.pdf

Packing Tips & Advice

What To Pack First

Start by packing shoes and heavier items at the bottom of the suitcase (by the wheels and/or where the luggage will lay flat on the ground). Clothing that's lighter or prone to wrinkling should be placed closer to the top; these are typically some of the last items to go in.

If you plan on collecting souvenirs or bringing home gifts, leave room in your luggage for these goodies.

Reducing Wrinkles

The topic of avoiding wrinkled clothing could be an entire chapter on its own, so I'm just going to briefly touch on various suggestions.

- Roll your clothes instead of folding them to avoid hard creases.
- If you prefer folding, put a piece of tissue paper or a plastic bag in the middle to help reduce wrinkles.
  - » For tissue paper, white is best just in case moisture gets into your luggage, which would cause colored tissue paper to stain your clothing.

> » When repacking at the end of the trip, the tissue paper can be repurposed to wrap various souvenirs which always seem to follow us home.

- Another option is to leave the clothes on hangers and cover them with dry cleaner bags. Then fold once and place into your suitcase.
- Pack clothing that's made of wrinkle-resistant fabrics such as polyester, microfiber, nylon, rayon or acrylic.

Fixing Wrinkles

Despite our best efforts it's nearly impossible to fully eliminate wrinkles. The above suggestions will help, but you'll probably still need to deal with a few wrinkles after unpacking. Besides ironing (it's unlikely your cruise line allows you to bring a clothes iron onboard), here are some other options:

- Downy Wrinkle Releaser spray that you can find in the travel size section of stores.
- Another wrinkle fix is a small spritzer. Fill it with hot water and thoroughly mist clothes.
- Some cruise lines offer 50% off clothes pressing on Day 1. Be sure to read their bulletin or you might miss out!

Dealing with Dirty Laundry

Pack either a couple of plastic bags or a collapsible laundry hamper. The hamper folds flat in your suitcase and the bags scrunch down into almost nothing.

Preventing Tangled Necklaces or Lost Earrings

A few suggestions for packing jewelry include:

- Taping necklaces or earrings to an index/recipe card
- Thin necklaces can be threaded through a drinking straw
- Organize earrings into one of those "daily pill containers"
- Buy a hanging jewelry organizer

Save Space by Making Your Wallet Smaller

Things you use on a regular basis while running errands around town won't be as useful while on a cruise. You probably don't need gas cards, certain loyalty program cards, club membership cards, etc. Put these aside in a safe place for when you return home.

Not to be pessimistic, but if your wallet gets lost/stolen that's already a big enough headache… and should you get hit with that bad luck, you'll have fewer things you need to replace.

Put Shoes Into Plastic Shopping Bags

This will help protect your clothing from dirt and street grime. Bonus points if they're bags from foreign stores so they can remind you of other fun places you've traveled!

Don't have any plastic bags since you reuse canvas shopping bags? Newspapers and flyers are frequently delivered in tube-like plastic bags (sleeves) which will fit over most shoes.

Efficient Shoe Packing

Unless we're talking about sandals, the fact of the matter is that shoes are bulky when compared to clothing; even if you have little feet. To address this problem, make efficient use of the inside of your shoes by stuffing them with the smaller odds and ends from your luggage. Socks are the top choice for this, but you could also pack shoes with underwear, undershirts, chargers and other small gadgets. The added benefit is that this stops shoes from getting crushed.

Efficient Shoe Storage

The answer to "How many shoes do you bring on a cruise?" is a personal one, ranging from as low as 2–3 (including flip flops) to more than a dozen. If you're the type that likes to have a good selection of footwear while on vacation, you're going to need a place to put all your shoes. They can clutter up your cabin and spill out of your closet.

Buy one of those shoe organizers, but not the over-the-door kind with pockets, I'm talking about the kind that hangs in a closet and has shelves. These are great for stashing shoes, small purses, and other small items. These shelf shoe organizers fold flat so they don't take up much space in your luggage.

Save Makeup Space

Using products that can multitask will help save space. For example, those 2-in-1 brushes with a large brush on one end and a narrow brush on the other end. Consider using a cream blush for some lip tint and maybe for eye makeup.

Don't bring your whole makeup collection, only bring items that will complement the clothes you're packing.

Protect Your Luggage from Rain

If there's a downpour while luggage is being loaded/unloaded from the plane or ship, then your clothes could get soaked. Even if it's not storming, maybe your luggage gets left on the tarmac for a while in the rain.

There are several ways to deal with this. On the inside, you can put your clothes into large clear plastic bags. On the outside, you can weather protect your luggage using a water repellent like Scotch Guard.

Luggage Reinforcement & Redundancy

R&R on your vacation definitely means rest & relaxation, but for your luggage it means reinforcement & redundancy. Not nearly as pleasant of a term, but necessary since luggage tags do come off.

It's hard to truly relax if your luggage is lost or delayed.

Don't let a missing tag be the cause of this. Use cable ties to reinforce the tags with those elastic strings. In addition to your permanent luggage tags, use all the tags provided by the cruise line and attach them on to different handles of your suitcase if possible.

Use luggage R&R to ensure that you get your own R&R.

How to Weigh Your Luggage

If your vacation involves a flight before or after your cruise, I recommend checking the airline requirements for your luggage. The allowed weights might be different for domestic vs international flights.

Knowing this ahead of time and weighing your luggage can save you the trouble of having to remove items at the airport or paying a hefty baggage fee.

The easiest method to weigh your luggage is to use a handheld luggage scale. This little accessory has a hook or clip which you attach to the handle of your suitcase. When you lift up the suitcase by grabbing the luggage scale it will display the weight of whatever's hanging from it.

The other option is to use a bathroom scale. This takes some more effort and math, but it's an option if you don't own a handheld luggage scale and don't want to buy one.

First you step on the scale while holding your suitcase. Write down that number. Then you step on the scale normally (without your suitcase) and write down that number. Finally, subtract the second number from the first number and you'll have the approximate weight of the suitcase.

Assorted Tips

- Fight stale smelling clothing by tucking a few fabric softener sheets between items.
- Pack some outfits in your travel companion's bag (and a couple of theirs in yours). In case of lost luggage, you'll have some fresh clothes to wear until your luggage catches up.
- Put toiletries in zip lock bags because sometimes they leak.
- If you like sending postcards you can prepare stick-on labels with the addresses already written on them. This will save precious vacation time and eliminate the need to bring a bulky address book.
- If you're packing any "adult toys", take the batteries out so they don't accidentally turn on and make your luggage seem like a bomb. This will prevent you from having an embarrassing run in with security.
- Roll up your belt and place it inside of the collar of a dress shirt. This will help keep the shirt collar stiff.

Just Say No to "Just In Case"

It's so easy to keep packing more things just in case you'll need them. There's an old traveler's saying about overpacking. The gist of it is:

Before closing your suitcase you should take out half of what you think you'll need.

If you're following my advice then you probably don't need to remove half, but when you're done packing do consider removing one outfit and adding more money.

ACCESSORIES TO MAKE LIFE EASIER

You probably don't need to bring ALL of these items, but here's a list of accessories and how they can help make cruise life easier. Pick and choose which to bring on your trip.

Inflatable Laundry Hangers

Even if you don't plan on doing laundry during the cruise, these will help dry out your swimsuit faster.

Inflatable hangers dry out clothes faster because they separate the fabrics allowing air to flow. They also reduce the need for ironing and it's great that they fold flat when not in use. Here are a couple options: Inflatable Laundry Hangers via Amazon.com and Scrubba inflatable hangers.

Plus, sometimes you just need extra hangers, especially on longer cruises.

Binoculars

Binoculars are a popular accessory to bring along for Alaskan voyages but are helpful during other cruises too. They can be used to view land animals, glaciers, whales, dolphins, seals, and even lava flows!

In addition to wildlife and nature, binoculars can also be used during excursions to see the details of cathedrals, artwork, and architecture. Lastly, some cruisers even like using them onboard to spot friends or children from a distance.

Hair Dryer

On some ships, every cabin comes with a hair dryer. On others, only certain suites get this amenity. And some ships don't provide hair dryers at all. If this accessory is important to you, check with your cruise line to find out what your situation will be.

However, even if your cabin comes with one, some people complain that the provided hair dryer is weak (e.g. Carnival says theirs are 1250 watts) so you may want to bring your own.

Packing Organizers (aka Packing Cubes)

I love having things organized so I think these are great; especially lightweight ones. Some people say they don't need packing organizers and that's fine; however, the packing cubes give you an advantage if airport or cruise security wants to inspect your luggage. With the packing cubes it's easy for security to search your bag without making a giant mess of everything, and you'll probably be finished with the inspection faster.

Space Bags to Compress Clothes

If you're going to use space saver bags, get the ones that don't require a vacuum. Put your clothes in carefully to minimize wrinkling and maybe have some wrinkle release spray ready for when you hang up the clothes afterwards.

Be aware that even though your clothes now take up less space, they'll still weigh the same!

Alarm Clock

Unlike hotels, most cruise cabins don't have an alarm clock. So, you can either bring your own or use your smartphone. To avoid roaming charges put your phone in airplane mode (this saves battery too).

Duct Tape

This versatile tool can fix anything from uncooperative luggage to annoying clingy shower curtains. You don't have to bring the whole roll, you can wrap a lesser amount around a marker or an old plastic card.

Some people prefer painter's tape instead because it doesn't leave behind a sticky residue like duct tape, and can be reused.

2-way Radios

These were more popular before widespread WiFi coverage and smartphones. However, if you don't want to pay for an onboard WiFi package, walkie talkies can help you stay in contact with your friends or family onboard. Please set the volume on low so that you don't disturb your fellow passengers.

Post-It Notes

A pad of sticky notes can be handy to leave messages for your friends, family, or cabin steward.

Translation Books or Apps

These are especially useful in Europe, where the itineraries are often filled with ports of various countries and languages.

Although many people who work in tourist areas do speak some English, it's nice to be able to say some basic phrases in the local language. Plus, if you venture off the beaten track you'll be more likely to need the translation help.

Rubber Band

A little trick some people recommend is putting a rubber band around your wallet to make it harder for pickpockets to lift it.

The idea is that the sticky band makes it harder to knock your wallet out of your pocket.

However, I've read that unfortunately this actually makes it easier to slip the wallet out of your pocket since the elastic band makes it smaller by compressing it.

Instead, you can reduce pickpocket success by carrying your wallet in the front pocket and/or turning it sideways.

Hand Sanitizer

A little bottle of germicidal hand cleaner could be a useful item to take on adventure excursions where water might not be readily accessible. It's no good getting sick during your vacation!

Moleskin

Great for blisters or broken skin. Unless you plan on lounging at the pool/beach all day every day, you'll probably be doing a lot of walking. Even with your most comfortable shoes you might develop a blister, and a moleskin patch will do the trick.

Medkit

For minor cuts and scratches, pack a small first aid kit with antibiotic cream and bandages. This is especially useful if you have kids or just tend to be accident prone.

Hat (Sun Protection)

Too much sun contributes to wrinkles, dark spots, and skin cancer. Protect your neck, ears, face, and scalp by wearing a hat.

Socks

Some people prefer to go barefoot, so much so that they don't even pack socks (especially if heading to warm destinations). It's probably a good idea to bring at least 1 pair in case you need them for specific activities like bowling or bungee trampolining.

Insulated Mug (with a lid)

Use the beverage station of the buffet area to fill your mug and your drinks will stay hot or cold with the lid on.

Small Flashlight and/or Nightlight

A mini flashlight will help you find your way (or dropped items) in the dark. It's also nice to have in case of an emergency.

Similarly, a nightlight allows you go to the bathroom without blinding yourself with the room light. It can also help a young one go to sleep.

Power Converter

Many cruise ships offer both North American and European electrical outlets, but hotels do not. If you have some overnights before or after your cruise, bring along a power converter. Then during the cruise you'll get an extra outlet since you can use the foreign outlet that you wouldn't normally be plugging into.

Tote Bag

Tote bags are versatile and lightweight. See if you can get one that folds up compactly into its own pocket.

Luggage Straps

I'm surprised I don't see these more often when traveling. The brightly colored straps make your suitcase easier to spot on the luggage carousel, secure your bag's contents while it's being tossed around during transit, and have buckles which can be quickly opened when access is needed.

WHAT NOT TO PACK

L uggage weighing in a little heavy? Suitcase bursting at the seams? Maybe you've packed some of these items which you don't need or aren't even allowed to bring.

Note: These are just guidelines. Your cruise line will have the final say and it's best to refer to their policies beforehand.

Over-the-door Shoe Organizer with Pockets

A common tip is to bring an over-the-door shoe organizer so that you can store stuff in all the pockets. From my research it seems that many cruise lines don't welcome this accessory because the hooks damage the top of the door.

Instead, use the closet hanging shoe organizer with shelves which I mentioned in the previous chapter on Packing Tips. It hangs from the rod in the closet so it won't cause that problem but still gives you organized storage space.

Beach Towels

Towels are provided by the cruise line. Thank goodness because they take up a lot of space in my suitcase!

Beer and Liquor

For many people BYOB is a way of life, but on a cruise ship you'll need to buy alcohol on-board. However, you're usually allowed to pack sealed wine (I'd suggest wrapping it in a t-shirt to give it some padding). Check with your cruise line for their limits on how much wine you can bring and any corkage fees for consuming outside of your cabin (e.g. the dining room, etc.).

Too Many Books

There's nothing like getting lost in a good book, especially while on vacation when you can let the time pass by without a care. However, bringing too many books will weigh you down and take up space.

An e-reader device or app might be the solution. If you want the real thing, then prioritize a few top choices, in this case paperback beats hardcover. Later, if you still need more to read you can visit your ship's library or go hunting in a local bookstore in port.

Coffeemaker or Kettle

A coffee maker might not be the first thing that comes to mind when packing for a cruise, but for a lot of people making coffee is the first thing they do when they wake up. In general, passengers are not allowed to bring electric items that produce heat.

Heating blankets, hot plates, and immersion heaters are other examples of items with heating elements that are usually prohibited.

Flat irons I've seen as both prohibited and allowed, so, as always, check with your cruise line.

Candles, Incense, Hookahs

These are also prohibited fire hazards.

Clothes Iron

Irons (and usually steamers) are basically banned industry-wide. With hundreds or thousands of people on a single ship, the cruise lines are unwilling to risk a fire. A few lines have self-service launderettes with ironing boards, but for those that don't you should be prepared to handle wrinkles using the tips from earlier in this book (see "Reducing Wrinkles" and "Fixing Wrinkles" in the chapter Packing Tips & Advice).

Extension Cord / Power Bar

Many people have said that they've had theirs confiscated, while others made it on-board. So, your mileage may vary. For those who need an extension cord to plug-in a CPAP machine, it's possible to get special permission for medical reasons.

Knives

Swiss army knives aren't technically banned on cruises, but there's a chance that whoever's working airport or ship security that day will have a problem with it. Pretty much everything you need on the cruise will be taken care of for you, so why risk getting on security's bad side? If you do decide to bring one, make sure the blade is small (less than 4 inches / 10 cm; restrictions may very).

Concealed bladed weapons are a different story. Those aren't welcome on airplanes or cruise ships.

Weapons

No firearms, firearm replicas, crossbows, stun devices, spears, explosives are allowed. The same goes for other projectile weapons such as paintball guns or air/BB/pellet guns.

Items for Port Use Only

There are some items that you can bring onboard but can't use onboard; they're for port use only.

The following list provides some examples. Please refer to your specific cruise company's guidelines for a complete list.

Carnival Cruise Line's List of "Items For Port Use Only":
- Drone Cameras
- Snorkel gear
- Segways
- Skateboards
- Golf clubs
- Fishing rods
- Tennis rackets
- Kites
- Roller blades or skates
- Collapsible Wagon *
- Metal detectors
- Boogie Boards (maximum 42 inches in length)
- Beach chair
- Umbrella
- Portable Folding Bicycles (maximum 20 inch tires)

* Collapsible wagons cannot be rolled onto or off of the ship

Lastly, check your children's carry-on because you never know what those little smugglers will try to sneak on vacation!

IMPORTANT NOTE: Each cruise line will have its own guidelines for which items are allowed on board their ships. Your luggage will be put through security and/or customs checks so please follow the policies of your cruise line, airline, and transportation security administration.

CONCLUSION

I hope this book has provided real value to you and that your vacation is full of smooth sailing. If you have any questions, suggestions, or tips you want to share, please send them my way.

I welcome your comments at book.feedback@kylerayim.com.

Reviews are like gold to authors! If you found this book helpful, or even if you didn't, please consider leaving an honest review on Amazon.

Thank you!

Made in United States
North Haven, CT
24 August 2023

40722591R00039